The Senderos

About the Author

Danny founded, directed, acted and wrote for two theatre companies during his career teaching Drama, English and Philosophy in London and Munich.

Upon retiring he found more time to apply himself to his writing. *The Senderos* is a product of this, as too are twenty plays, twelve of which have been produced professionally.

Currently he lives in the West Country, although he spends a significant part of the year in Andalucia.

Apart from writing and theatre, he enjoys walking, reading, sailing and spending time with his family.

The Senderos

A Journey of the Mind

Danny Strike

Copyright © 2020 Danny Strike

The moral right of the author has been asserted.

Apart from any fair dealing for the purposes of research or private study, or criticism or review, as permitted under the Copyright, Designs and Patents Act 1988, this publication may only be reproduced, stored or transmitted, in any form or by any means, with the prior permission in writing of the publishers, or in the case of reprographic reproduction in accordance with the terms of licences issued by the Copyright Licensing Agency. Enquiries concerning reproduction outside those terms should be sent to the publishers.

Matador
9 Priory Business Park,
Wistow Road, Kibworth Beauchamp,
Leicestershire. LE8 0RX
Tel: 0116 279 2299
Email: books@troubador.co.uk
Web: www.troubador.co.uk/matador
Twitter: @matadorbooks

ISBN 978 1838594 640

British Library Cataloguing in Publication Data.
A catalogue record for this book is available from the British Library.

Printed and bound in Great Britain by 4edge Limited
Typeset in 11pt Adobe Garamond by Troubador Publishing Ltd, Leicester, UK

Matador is an imprint of Troubador Publishing Ltd

To Lynda, Jamie and Lucy in thanks for their love and support.

Contents

The Gesture	1
Cosh	2
Sour Love	3
The Me And They Of It	4
Toy Room Dynasties	5
Inner Chimp	6
Reincarnation	7
A White Tree	8
Lady In Sevilla	9
Lonely	10
Plymouth Sound	11
My Boat	12
The In And Out Of Cake	13
Time Heals?	15
Oblivion	16
Watching The Diving	17
Off Centre	19
Missed It	20
School Matters	21
Still Life	23
Cave Painter	25
Where Have All The Angels Gone?	28
True Love	31
Upon Meeting Lynda	32
Mother Tongue	33
Jellyfish	35
Kate Walks The Night	36
Cement	39
Swimmer	41
Valentine	42
Philosopher's Pond	43
Founder's day	44
Yes	46
Meeting	47
Getting Old	48
Starts The Day	49
Post-Modern	50
Figurehead	52
Nefertiti	53
Parrot	54
Perfect Poem	55
Grey Days	57
They've Murdered A Good Murder	58
Morning Ponder	60
Morning Drunk	61
Island Church	62
Coffee Comfort	63
Life's Wheal	64
Friend Dying	65
On The Balcony	67
Sierra Moment	68
Portrait Of King In Sevilla	69
Parting	70
A Corner Unnamed	71
Cheetah	72
The Wall	73

Scavenger	74
Safe?	75
Wind Farms	76
Post	77
At The Beach Bar	78
Pete	79
Muslim Woman Floating	81
Nun	82
Fishing	83
Drowned Fox	84
Lewis In A Tangle	85
Nan	87
Micro Assassin	88
The Going	89
Green Grave	90
Going To The Match	91
Another White Tree	92
Hornpipe	93
Woodland Meeting	94
Amoeba Prayer	96
Breakfast	97
Basta!	98
Casting Flowers	99
Curator	100
Will Rising	101
Inflatable	102
The Bride	103
Wound	104
On The Death Of My Friend	105
Spy	106
On The Tube	108
One-Man Universe	109
Old	110
Squashed At The Station	111
A Promise	112
Information Desk	113
Late Infidelity	115
Doves	116
Old Love	117
Boat	118
Glass Of Water	120
Last Thought	121
The Senderos	122

The Gesture

A boy, faded shorts, pale skin, sharp ribs,
sun-salt hair, relishes the suck of
tide in his toes, but frowns.
Sun in eyes? No, older than his years,
more a shiver DNA sent,
suspicion of a future not so good,
a knotty one will take some getting through.

Idly waves plastic spade, swatting nothing.

He'll use that gesture through the years:
facing students, marrying, falling in love,
rowing with self at garden end,
looking on a newborn, divorcing,
marrying again.

Some mystic pass, superstitious cipher,
paddler's signal – all's well,
but might not be, or it's not so good
but getting better.
No, shit, I'm drowning!
Forget it.

And dying he'll make it,
a tad relieved, some regret
but what the hell, it's done.

Cosh

Thought's a cosh!
You spilt it! You stole it! You said it!
Did! Did! Did!
You done it shithead, scrambled egg head,
sour slop-in-the-bin head.
Rogue thought, rampant, pell-mell Judas thought
playing at muddledom, at peek and boo with
constant bias for the best-forgot, like an old boot
nudging an animal corpse to make the maggots mill.
Coshing! Coshing! Coshing!

Sour Love

There's a thin affection for a thief
I keep for her. Pulled it off. Away clean.
Her hurt? She spoiled? No, mine the grief.
Knifed, razored, gutted neat and clean;
Slow lick along my spine, fingering groin.
I'd have died swearing her soft and sure,
Hip to hip, loin on loin, knew her for true coin.
But she was cold core, ultimate whore!
She'd work one with all the hum and thrum
Of practised player, virtue's daughter,
Virgin's shudder, new to climax and come,
But not her the lamb, nor her the slaughter.
Sometimes of a night alone and sadding
I hear in empty home her pad, pad, padding.

The Me And They Of It

For I am everyone and she is me
or I am nothing, an empty shell,
a dying bloom.
I have felt cinder beneath my feet,
the tape upon my breast,
strode the stage in many roles,
touched a first worrying sore,
awaited the bullet in the neck,
been Fool and General,
Lover and Left.

Without this compass
there is no reach,
no breath worth drawing,
no thought worth form.

Toy Room Dynasties

Prowling puppets
Leave no trails;
Ripped teddies
Tell no tales.

Inner Chimp

i am the chimp
the telltale wrinkle
the baggy eye
that dull headache
the thought that never sleeps
phantom breath on your neck
sudden fall in a dream
a silent scream
in your head
i can spy and seek
coming ready or not.

Reincarnation

My plumber's mate believes in reincarnation
so when his head is not hidden by a drain
he reads Euripides, Sophocles and Aristophanes
and dreams of being a Greek writer again.

A White Tree

Surely such a tree never grew!
Coming, sudden on the bow,
out of a turn in tide turbulent river,
brazen beneath a storm sullen sky.

A vision of a tree, bright white,
biblical promise and threat,
naked and stark as first woman;
an Eve of a tree, prophesy full,
flaring amidst lush dark green.

A work of modern art,
three odd angled branches,
not a leaf, sanded and painted
virginal pure, but bearing totems:
head crushed doll,
angel with a face lisp and
perky monkey hanging, noosed.

Lady In Sevilla

Cool and pale,
ear pearled proud profile,
dramatic mascara, loud rouge lips,
smooth wound turban,
jewelled pins thrust in like magician's swords.

So she sits,
her blue gown a palimpsest of muted mosaics
to which sunlight clings
as if to a dancer it might lose.

She bends, long fingers
offering bird pecking in the dust
a crisp.
It shivers, retreats, she perseveres, it disdains,
she smiles and desists
as if to say,
the best of the day is done.
I'll undress now and lay in a soft breeze.

Lonely

Not so much your absence.
That's given,
but the sudden cold shock
when of a day I think
I'll tell her that later
over wine, beer or coffee.
Then have to remember
again and again and again:
you're gone.

Plymouth Sound

In this dawn's pressing stillness
the long grey slabby waves roll
ominous and endless
beneath a bright pitching
orange buoy zany and sharp.

My Boat

Clasp knife silver with marlin spike, shackle key, blade.
Apple, firm, shiny, green and red, copper brindled.
Pink pork pie, gelatinous beneath moist crust.
Boat bouncing as uneven swell runs beneath,
sails rattling in a capricious wind.
Fickle day of gust and pause;
fragile sun through scurrying cloud threatening storm.
Time yet to finish.
Last burst of burnt tasting beer,
chew pie, tongue crust,
cut, blade to thumb, a neat slice of apple.
Drop off the wind,
catch a homeward tide.

The In And Out Of Cake

Pausing
outside gleaming glass doors,
long steel tubular handles,
opened by a uniform.

Soft torso,
white suit city blotched,
thin hair drifting in the wind,
he sits,
hands folded, one on other, palms up.

The crowd churns past.

His pusher
fumbles with wheelchair brake,
breathing heavy, foot clubbed, face spotty.
Gently strokes his friend's head.
He smiles,
or rather a tremor passes over his gaunt face
and sinks away like sugar in a vat.

Through the mirror clean doors,
uniform opened,
a world of neatly ranged cakes,
sculpted, doilied and plated,
red, pink, slate grey, glazed white,
laurelled with cool creamy coils
squeezed deft on snow smooth icing,
layered strawberries, cherries,
apple slices, burnished plums
beneath gleaming jelly on sponge bases
light and yellow as a child's sun.

The cake eaters mouth gently,
blow soft ripples across creamy coffee,
bolstered on all sides by walls of blue
and classic triangles above sylvan ovals.

They are precise
in neat suits, lacy dresses and flouncy hats.

The crowd churns by; the friends push on.

Time Heals?

You cheated, not the usual way – another
woman, a hidden child, that I could have
handled, maybe, but not your leaden libido
and the jaunty wearing of it.
Nobody in 1968 said, let's wait.
And I, classic haughty flake, emancipated
sixties woman, huh! thought
how novel, he respects me, loves me.
Not the crushed behind a sofa, Cohen dregs,
wine gone kind, but true love.
Too late the coward limped out from swagger,
not fair, the scared heart. See how quick
I am, even now at this late year, to reach
for the knife – remember?

Oblivion

Take the question,
can you imagine oblivion?
No.
I don't buy it.
It's not a sleep, a passing out, a coma.
No, it won't do.
There will always be a crack,
a flick of the veil,
a peep backstage,
a glimpse of future doings
five hundred years hence. Five million!
There will always be some sort of Me.
Some nano micro shudder,
a step on the grave, a flutter of the soul,
an unexplained chill or sudden itch
at the edge of the universe
in some dense black hole,
as small as it can get
and still be called ongoing:
I'll know.

Watching The Diving

Pin precise and seamless it is not,
the imperfect dive of no poise or profile
and garbled blash heard
by small boy at some distance.
In red T-shirt, blue shorts, plastic sandals
clutching a green boat, stood by a bin,
over full and taller than him,
turns and takes in
the sun faded lawns and the scatter of
oiling
reading
ball playing
scolding
eating
sleeping islands.

Better to stay by the bins and watch
the diving.

But then there's the tempting rocks
landscaped in heavy-duty plastic
embroidered by streams curving through
clusters of screaming children, streams
that finish in frenzied fountained pond
where maybe he'll launch his boat
but nearby, a wrinkled tan,
slopping belly, varicose veins,
white breast feeding – maybe not.

Better watch the diving.

Another dive, but it's not right,
one arm flaying oddly half way,
head askew, black hole of mouth
wide as the water gobs it.

Off Centre

Everything was off:
new house slowly giving up faults,
a rumble in the heating,
a plaster weakness,
hair standing awkward in the mirror,
partner loved and loathed,
children inheriting fault lines.

An elbow nudge, accident or?
Was that a smile or grimace?
Wait a while, but all's so 'so, so'.
All so Yesno.

So much stuff through filters:
fatigue, hope, shall I?
Next time, try harder.
Will you ever?
Will you?

Missed It

A shadow on the pavement,
a knock on the old inn door,
headlights in the branches,
all a waste of held breath,
cliched crap!
The trap is laid,
the honied steel teeth of
romance, riches and adventure
offered but blunted as days
plod by.

There must have been one
better baited.

School Matters

There was no massacre today.
The school was the same
Victorian brick and long windows,
the playground tarmac sport marked,
students a motley of shoving friendly cheek,
or lolling extravagant, cool, disdainful.
No, there was no massacre today
but there was an announcement!
All staff at mid-morning break.
There the head.
Short, big tie, pinching loose neck
and 'So and So' to be expelled.
'So and So'?
Certainly no thick thug or Oxbridge hopeful.
Ah yes, 'So and So'!
One with eyes that looked right through,
made a fist of the average.
Gun found with list in his bedroom.

No, there was no massacre today,
just the hint of one. And the list?
Some staff asterisked –
to be shot? Or spared?
An invite to know alone in head's office.

Do I want to? There's the question?
If to be shot? Was it my humour, tone,
a tired reprimand, satiric barb?

To be spared? Perhaps a kindness,
a winning word, a smile.

Or perhaps just not marked.
A shadow who prowled a room a while,
tried to impart this and that and such,
not worth the bother –
just collateral, or not.

Still Life

Photos lie, that's a truth.
See here, the bloodsucker sun
would fry flesh dry.

For sure!
She'd have herself well done.

Eyes? Those globs?
Each a cotton dab
steeped and strained in acetate,
gave the skin a sudden thrill,
left a sweet cleaner smell.

In the glass there by her side.
With finger and thumb she'd tong it,
soft and lank, plop it on eyeball.
Perfect fit, mushy neat.

Her mascara? Sure she wore it.
Amazing you should ask.
From hotel, house or chalet,
not a step sans mask, face new wombed.
Ah how she'd paint proud, scour skin, fist flesh,
grind and groan, collapse on cycle with a lover's moan,
not a stitch of flesh her own.
All product of a surgeon could cut and suck a gland,
bring bloom to breast, turn white to tan.

Prided herself on her dress? My god, yes!
As a younger woman had some taste,
chose clothes of colour not plain or mute
but with flow and form decidedly cute.
Alas no more, see here, all gone to waste.

Yes always in high heels,
kicked off beside those books.

No, not a reading woman really.
Liked a good story but often tired.
Carried her books, more like her oils,
totems, priestly doings.

Here this shot has it. The high heels
thin, quavering, strapless, like her bra,
tightened her calves, gave form to bum.
But it all went soft, fruited, bruisey.

Boozy? Ha, ha! Yes…
Her eyes? Pretty. Quite.

Cave Painter

From sun baked mountains
mottled by slow cloud shadows,
she emerges pink almond trees haloed
nearly at journey's end;
fingers the damp sand, reading,
as she read the soil around
endless campfires where more
felt than seen ancient kin fed her –
chosen voyager.

She enters the lake,
lean of muscle, sinew,
tendon tight and bone proud,
corpse pale but for black hair and crotch patch,
high stepping until wading, the cold water
lapping the heat off her but not
quenching the burn within.

Finally,
she strikes out, just a sleek head,
a neck held bundle of skins,
a mouth full of colour.

A hawk pauses, loops down, notes
nothing more than a simple human head.
But
witness the nearby medieval bridge
propped and buttressed to hold
a dreary stream of modern traffic.

One must dream the other.
Both cannot be in the same
time held space; space held time
except in ancient knowing
where stones dream, soils speak
and airs whisper.
                    All clear to the
jumping fish moiling in her wake,
the claque of scuttering duck
escorting her on;
                    clear even to
the returning hawk reeled back
by instinct stronger than hunger.

So she skewers time, the touch
of her stroke not felt by heavy
flannelled bather,
                    nor king's messenger
urging his horse right through her.

Landed and clad, she hears the
ground tell her listening feet
of echoic darks
where she'll squeeze her pliant self,
chew pigments
to orange, ochre and radiant gold,
spit
a limning glow around
drooled fingertip dabbed
animal and long one-armed
spear-bearing warrior,
then rest an aeon,
corpse certain.

Where Have All The Angels Gone?

Nobody's put up much of a fight for angels,
no extinction warriors, no massing crowds
from Trafalgar Square to the Palace.
Fair enough, I suppose,
we're quieter these days, more personal,
but come on, we did have style!
Who stopped Abraham's hand that time?
Who rolled back the tombstone?
Say it myself, we were doing alright, and then
THE BIG ONE! – A VIRGIN BIRTH!
And it was that birth changed everything.
Trumpets, heavenly voices, gone.
That's all Old Testament,
O.T. as we call it.
Somebody starts getting above themselves,
acting flashy, O.T. we chant.
Yes that birth changed everything big time.
We became more subtle, discreet,
working on the inside so to speak,
prompting, whispering kindness, compassion.
So next time you help a stranger,
or buy a Big Issue, give to a food bank,
think on.

But part of me misses the old days.
How word would go round
and we'd throng, all bustle and expectation,
waiting for one to land soft and sure
swooping out of the blue in seamless glide –
full of it.
You should have seen those Babylonians,
well into the pork and wine,
weapons, shields careless against the walls,
floor loot strewn, wenching kicking off,
and as for Belshazzar!
Purple faced, well whored,
pipers and drummers giving it craic.
What did you do? we chorused.
I went for it:
cold wind, drapes shivering, whiff of burnt sand,
crack of lightning and my disembodied hand
writing on the plaster fresco style
with an Arabic flourish:
Belshazzar,
"You have been weighed and found wanting."
Then, Wow! And Wow again! and Hallelujah Wow!
Flinging ourselves up, looping the loop,
splashing the cloud stuff and passing the ambrosia.
But there's me getting all O.T.

No, let's face it,
a drunk fed at a shelter,
a rough sleeper housed,
an abused child fostered,
that's worth more than
all your flaming swords,
blazing garments, polished haloes,
so let them rust, grow damp, fade,
but spare a thought for angels.

True Love

On the rump of the music
beneath the louring house,
their long shadows merging
over the rocky terrace, motlied in
capricious light, they descend
damp steps, pass beneath grim greek
statues and moon etiolated grass,
pause a pause, tongue-tied
at the immensity of what they do.
They crouch,
push back whippy branches,
reach the pressed boat.
The black river suspires regretfully,
not heard!
So conspires true to its part,
as too the darkening moon.
Only the humid stillness of the
coming storm sighs true note –
ignored!
All weary witness to love's
stunning surprise
and its future stalking demise.

Upon Meeting Lynda

You may as well play $e=mc^2$ for laughs
with all your scopes and countless graphs.
You men of learning, you men of thought,
truth's eluded you, for lovers have wrought
a fresh alphabet, a new turned key
and bottled the breath of eternity.

So give over your weights, measures and rules,
let grammar go wince, leave logic to fools
for only love and next to love art
can show us the trick of it – the heart.

Mother Tongue

Her back bruising on a warehouse wall
beneath stern cranes, louring black tankers
she mingled a moment's grim passion
with his garlic sweat and
traded one slum for another.

She thought
the earth move promising foreign parts,
clear mountain moons, silky jungle whispers,
dawns from nights of love.
But nothing moved, only bleak greasy
creatures shadow shaped slipping across
dock stones.

He married her.
They deported him.
She went.
Poor Dot.
Made her bed.
But foreign.
Nought here for her.
Even so.
Don't know what'll come of it.
Have you mashed that tea?

Ahora, a tooth cracked, squint eyed
Madonna looks on in Rio back streets
at a black hunched woman
sat on indelible stamped crate –
Producto de Espana – in mourning,
not for her pot-bellied, scratching lover,
nor the extra seven he gave, two dead,
one gone, others round about trailing
a scatter of grandchildren, but for
a lost tongue.

Jellyfish

Surely not native here
but pulsed from some
other world?
At whim of wave and
current caprice they
cast no shadow but a
sting.

Kate Walks The Night

I absconded.
Home? Hospital? Prison?
Sectioned I think…
Followed in my sister's footsteps.
No, avoided them.
Killed on a slip road she was.
So trudge.
Awake, asleep? No idea.
I walk in fear, no, not true.
Fear death?
Think I've got cancer.
Not me, my psychosis.
Maybe why they locked me up.
Nobody's locked up for insomnia.
That's not a crime.

Somewhere I started a sketch.

Then a burning hand on my shoulder.
Cancer hand?

Wander for hours.
Play games.
Approaching person?
Play androgyny.
Walk bow-legged.
Hunch and swagger
trying for no sex.
So's she? He?
I'm not afraid to be attacked.

I drew a stick figure.
Young women will steal if they can.

There's a dog on my chest,
sweaty, drooly.

I'm not scared but my psychosis is terrified,
bowel stuck, sweat on back of legs, throat rigid.

I starved, stole a pickled egg.
Ever tried that?
Soft, gooey, slides about.
Took some snatching.
Snuck up on a chip van.
Did it! High five!

Begged for hours
not far from that slip road.
A few insults.
A man talked and talked and talked
of Abyssinia.
Have we had a war there?
Another gave me 4 x 2ps.
What's that all about?

Had a row a thousand years ago.
Man/husband/flirt/
onenightram@fuckedup.com

Couldn't sleep.
Girl opposite would steal him.

So we sketched,
trying to out etch the other,
not daring to sleep
and my charcoal stick
twisted and turned,
broke and crumbled
until the whole sheet was
a mind made mess.

Cement

He kisses gently on her crinkly lips,
licks a fingertip, dabs a mascara flake.
She smiles, teeth long and yellow,
eyes greying, blood flecked,
runs her fingers in his lank beard
presses a spot or two.

So they love, old to old,
slipping through surfaces.

A boy, a girl, a bar,
he, pocketing change, drops
jaunty beside her, takes her hand
or was that later?

No hint of howling times
rather time to pet and pant,
build love's scaffold
with this and that, routine matters,
little habits, minor irritants and
cement their certainty.

But oh, for the boy and the dance
and howling time done.

So comes on the evening,
kept down with tired T.V.,
until the long night howl.
His from eternity and hers
raking up through shrunk
flesh and bone, and she would
be gone, but promised.

A promise too to keep the place up.
So by day she paints skirting,
polishes tiles, emulating his proud way.
Would cement up plaster cracks
as one ices cakes, but
doesn't trust cement.

Swimmer

She wears wet red, sheds it simple,
peeling and stepping and reaching to peg.
The taut cut of her buttocks, calves, breast
an erogenous cameo as all around blazes:
magnolia, orange blossoms, oleander cascades.

Valentine

You are my silken thread.
You are the shawl slipping
through an old trader's ring.
You are the bedspread balled
to a fist, released to
float crease-free before
a tourist's awe.
You are
things delicate and fine,
lasting and fast.
I love you.

Philosopher's Pond

In flowery light pink,
a woman poses,
flip flops in one hand,
sunglasses hanging from
her skinny cleavage,
at the philosopher's pond,
murky, lily-leafed, occasional
slow roll of gold-backed fish.
She wants her toes in
the fountain jet.
He crouches;
she bends back, beams,
toes ready, hand behind head.
Now!
She topples and
for a second's shutter click
her face is hers,
not tired tourist trying
but pixie, wrinkles alive,
eyes surprised, laughing
at her foot plonk…That's the photo.

Founder's day

They're all there:
clergy, local business, parents.
Teas drank, beer tent stuttering,
bunting not so sprite,
ladies' hats listing,
breeze turning chill.

Boys versus Old Boys creaking to a close.
Draw a fair bet, but last man in,
more an afterthought to fill the tail,
holds his own, scores a steady twenty,
sparks a flagging day.

Pints held tense, silence for each ball.
The bishop and others watch now,
as too boys rumoured in from woods.

He a third man, carrier of drinks,
a lifelong mantel already laid,
prompter, sub, run an errand,
go a spell or two…
He to turn the day?

He watches the heavy angered bowler
lope in and deliver an ill-tempered ball.
Never forgot the clean smack,
a winning boundary before it left the bat,
and the thought, it doesn't get better than this.
And it didn't.

Yes

There must have been a moment
when all was foretold.
A glimpse into a stilled pond,
done a thousand times before, but
this once awesome.
An ancient shocked
knew that hewasHe, or shewasShe
and allwasI and
Science and Art were birthed.

Meeting

She enters complete with mahogany stick,
glass topped.
Hair blonde, cut theatre curtain style,
presents her face.
Cat black mascara, purple lips, dress
precisely chosen.
No faltering fold or puckered pleat,
all seamed aright.

The other waits, blingy, does not rise,
rolls her jellied eyes, lifts e-cigarette,
wrist cocked, indicates with green nails
the leather-backed phone, allows a tremor
to cross her smooth face as if to say,
I'm held. Heard it all, but you know!
Then done, click. Why hi!

They embrace fragile, kiss air, cheeks not touching.

Getting Old

Is not so bad.
Now is your time to
become a tidal thing,
rolling in, rolling out,
turning as planets do,
star gazing them out.
Then in the cool dawn,
smile, settle your head
and sleep until sunset.

Starts The Day

He, in ankle long coat, coffee done, rolls his paper.
She arrives sharp, white-black, neat plastic tiara perched.
He searches in purse, frowns – could he have? But no.
A wart, almost beautician placed, puckers as he smiles,
lays two crisp notes. She gathers, withdraws. He rises
steadily, defying coat's weight, gestures to another.
She at door holds hat of hunter's green could else be forgot.
He nods, slips a coin, leaves.

Post-Modern

A pregnant woman sat down beside me
as I read a wall of forward-looking poetry
painted large red on white –
shit fuck
get over it
asshole.

Did some forward-thinking of my own –
gentlemen never come first, are
erect as needed and will fit any grave.

She wore a light grey puli,
chunky cardigan, jeans, big boots;
rubbed her temples.

I studied a picture of a
bin with a broken brolly in.

She leant forward, screwed her face
as if to cry.

Are you O.K.?
I have a little headache,
if I can help,
thank you.

Then I walked in the gardens,
green swans and red tree,
a drum drooling over pie,
R squared that is.

And wondered what has post-syncretic realism ever done for me?

Figurehead

What a ship!
What a figurehead!
Plunging, thirsting deep through trough,
beauty arising from surf, foam flying,
wind flayed dry, so she plies, plunge and rise,
scoured and soaked, soaked and scoured.
Magic Latin blessed, curse free, garish torso,
arms bound back, hair gold,
eyes burning booty sure.

Nefertiti

Blot eye!
She's marred to a purpose,
blemish beauty becoming
in soft sand smooth face,
symmetrised by proud nose,
precise above deliberate red lips,
hint of smile reflected in
good blue eye, tear touched,
brow dolphin-backed.
Stunning crescendo of a face.

Parrot

Blue and black, green and gold,
fellow traveller, conspirator, mate
with a key in his gut.
He's known a thief parley,
a whore smoulder,
the lisp of a flatterer,
but none ever guessed,
thought nought of drowsy drunk,
his worn map,
nor his busy bird
but a brim full trunk was only
a scalpel cut away.

Perfect Poem

Between foot and step
the poet has slaved and failed.
So do not covet form or accident,
rather sit on a beach and forget
the words, words that block
lying like film, smear, veil.
Forget wave, surf, pebble, sand,
think that the first foot
did not need coarse, granular, fine,
nor tang, salt, roar, rattle
and all that followed –
sweeping and sighing alliterative assonance,
and the rest.

No, the perfect poem is not written.
I wrote that line and regretted it.
First the Platonist pondered,
he's right. We cannot escape the cave.
So I repeated myself.
The perfect poem is not written
and emphasised written.
Warump! cried the Modernist,
let it happen...

Tiring of centuries of struggle I wrote,
I am the first foot on the beach
and I tell you
words fail,
so here are
my foot-held
memories…
…
…
Even the dots are too much!

Grey Days

I live in fear of the grey days
sullen, strung in the trees,
squatting on drab fields,
frosted and hard mudded,
barren backdrop to
a slippery sea, spray lustless.

Days that gnaw at hope,
a time to come when you're gone
and I must strain to rise, cook, clean,
be busy, busying the pointless
to forget you gone.

Those future days girding
themselves in slow pounce.

They've Murdered A Good Murder

Gather the suspects, library;
candlesticks in the cellar and all that.
All changed.
Where's Holmes and a funny pipe,
frowning Watson, or smoothy Hercule?
Heaped over with trite formulaic M.Os.
A body found, muddier the better,
clothes on, off, in between.
Signs of sexual activity or?
Been there long? Not killed here.
Bored stroppy pathologist,
not my job but see what I can do.
Rogue detective, job's worth super.
So let's get to it you all.
Pictures on a glass wall,
arrows, notes and other scrawl.
Door to door to door, or?
We've a few questions, sorry but…
What are you suggesting?
Enemies? No. Never kill herself!
We have to ask.

See his bedroom? Of course.
We're no closer. Give her another try.
You think it's me! I'd like to have…
Path report's in. Somebody's not –
Pull him in.

Thank god for adverts and a snooze.

Who did it? No idea. Don't care.
Not the one with the gun, that's sure.
Oh how I miss the colonel in the study
with lead piping. Or the butler will do.

Morning Ponder

Scabby legs and pustuled face,
trussed in oversized white shorts,
T-shirt tight, a hay bale look,
he plods and pauses.
Faded eyes oblivious to
palm and cypress, oleander
flowering, bougainvillaea tumbling,
but strangely fascinated
by cracks in orange path,
as if some quotidian app
never quite happened for him.

Morning Drunk

Early morning Spanish street,
barred windows, studded doors, stone stepped.
Heat threatens cool silence.
Waiters cart out chairs, tables, others dampen cobbles.
Some movement to work,
neat women, leathered and bloused, sharp men, open shirts.
Suddenly out of one alley and into another, red shirt, floppy shorts, rushing ape gait forward falling, plump down, sat bent double,
hands full of head.
Two bespattered house painters haul him up, toes dragging,
mother him to a bench, turn his face, adjust a loose foot.
He sleeps.

Island Church

Wild place lone out crop white church red roof open to all winds centuries of rain solid seafaring faith graveyard a motley mix of lichened slabs epitaphs blurred pitted scrolls modernistic smooth stone clean loud lettering paunchy cupids blown cheeks perky trumpets sprays of flowers wild roses favoured…
Then the view,
across a yellow field distant masts.

Coffee Comfort

He drinks dark coffee
laced with quiet sorrows
next to a nouveau fountain
in a classic square
and thinks,
I have strode mountains,
sailed seas, and trod stages,
told a good story.

Life's Wheal

Broke-winged early
he attended all functions,
a shadow laughing.

Friend Dying

I look past her too bright eyes, past
her cancer and its narrowing intent,
past her potted plants, neat lawn.

The estuary's busy:
a tanker reverses, churns to berth,
sprite dinghies tack in new sunlight,
a cormorant dries its wings…

She'll give an odd chuckle, half gargle,
shrug, sigh, raise an eye as if to say
there are no more surprises.

Chemo abandoned, more harm than good,
so it's weeks, not months, maybe days.

Just mice gnawing at my bones.
On a bad night, I hope the painkillers win.

She's asked me a thousand times,
will I read at her funeral?
But hasn't said what –
you decide.
Liddles' catalogue then!
She'll raise a coughy laugh at that,
always one for a bargain.

Rising to go, I see a yacht,
sails shuddering as it tacks
for open sea and France.

On The Balcony

Black melon seeds.
Hardy little sods. Dropped? Spat?
On pink hibiscus.

Sierra Moment

Down the slate covered slope,
sprouting black burnt thistles,
a claw like scorched tree
clutches at blue sky.
Sudden! Crevice deep!
A spine of green trees
hugs an unseen river.

At the wet wooden bridge,
sunless beneath the trees,
grey grass hangs, stringy,
damp earth clinging,
like scalps.

Portrait Of King In Sevilla

Porno pious faces cauled in spicy
Torch lit incense, gothic framed,
Stylish in their pity, luxurious in
Vicarious ecstasy, a curled lip,
A forced tear and muffled grin.

In truth
Some pray, some turn away, but the mockers
Have it for there's a king to die, but he'll
Humble first. What better than a royal
Grovel and holy to wit?

Head yanked back, bald patch crowns
His long grey hair.
A bald king! Sweet giggle.
Neck roped, white smock, perfect.
Forced to stare at hovering host in
Well scoured thin prelate's fingers,
Chasuble shark-finned.

Nearby, neatly placed, a red carpet,
Crossed swords, a prostrate waiting lady,
A crown, a kneeling queen, plain gown,
Fingers just touching in hope-lost prayer as
Latin chant sours in her ears.

All three – king, queen, porno pious crowd wait.

Parting

They both felt bad: he for walking out,
she for trapping him. And they say
memory's uncertain, but not with shit guilt.

Drive by brain hits direct, dead eye
thought. Morning paper, chocolate
and bang! There she stands again,
eyes tear filled, begging a last embrace.

A Corner Unnamed

I like the unnamed best.
Take this empty corner,
leave it unnamed,
do not size it for
semantics, syllable or syntax,
let it be, see it as you will,
beautiful, sinuous, fine,
lithe in air, sure of space,
complete in form, rare in grace.
So put a portrait or a plant.
What's gained?
You've named it, tamed it.
Shame, for now you'll pass,
not notice, let it grow dust.

But leave it unnamed,
people it with dreams:
a crouching contrabandist,
child finger on lips,
a crying maidservant,
and you'll have
a corner of deep seams.

Cheetah

No mirage dare play on such eyes,
retinas retaining a thousand dusty
prints ancestral of thrashing cuddles
on baked mud or sun broken grass.
An algorithm of uncoiling cool fury,
aplomb of power, genes primed nuclear,
each line graph perfect.

Not so the grinning goon, craning forward,
fat belly burying curved railing,
tracksuit bottom rucked up bum,
greasy red anorak, lime green ski cap,
hissing himself hoarse in paltry parody.

Deaf to phlegmatic rumbling, presaging terror
that could spade a spine in blurred snap of claw;
snatch an idiot's eye, leave him constant token
of what it means to be a prisoner
when the free are not worth the gift.

The Wall

He trusted stone all his life.
Has a stiff backed walk, thigh heavy,
remnant of much lifting.
A hammer swing to his arms.
Always stops, beyond the village,
over the stile, other side of the stream,
presses a hand on the first wall he built.
Moves nearer, breaths in and marvels at
the cold smell, hidden beat of
scabrous stone, bold stone, shy stone,
stone seeds gifting to live mind.
His inspired eye can find helmet profile,
highlighted cheekbone blushing black,
arrow slit, a woman turning aside,
solo lichened tear.
In deeper damps
finds new a pockmarked chin,
a scarred eye,
mossy beard round smarmy mouth.
He knows his wall, old and fresh,
weathering time, working art
on stone-rooted palimpsests.

Scavenger

The road feeds me fox, doe, dog.
I don't kill.
I harvest, turning some stomachs.

Safe?

The pigeons are fat,
the squirrels sleek.

Night – easy badgers forage lazily
on close-cropped lawns,
hedged and edged and
bramble free.

Day – pedigree pups play.
But whose the hidden bike
all clobbered up with
wires, pliers, cosh
and black bag of bags?

Wind Farms

Silver silent winged ploughs,
no satanic mills or striding pylons
but gentle giants plying the air,
majestic in their unison,
harvesting power Art full.

Post

Chuttering to a stop astride an old bike
brakeless, but for foot on front tyre,
smiles, toothless, moustache nicotine caked,
one eye palled white; roots in heavy, listing
shoulder bag,
no, none for you, but there's the day,
and heaves on, away.

At The Beach Bar

He at the beach bar.
She, loose vest, bikini bottom, stocking tops.
Looks again!
Fifty years gone sudden as a sea gust,
he stands crushing her to him, her
buttoned blouse hard on his bare chest,
stroking her silk pants, fingering stocking line,
thumbs in suspenders, and she scratches,
digs gentle, long nailed into his back.

She with ice full glass turns away,
stocking tops a clever tattoo.
How will that wear with older skin?
How would Eileen have worn?

He's not done bad, lives with it.
His gin and tonic, bubbles tickling,
ice cracking, lemon zest biting,
first of the day.

Pete

He'll pass that wall daily, carton of milk,
newspaper for certain, hard hewn granite,
retained now, character for the estate beyond.
Bed wet wall, he'll think.
Father gone ahead and he to stay, Pete to fly.
Bed-wetting not a boarding-school favourite,
and he never did again.
But all's past, a pact with lumpy porridge,
kippers, streaky bacon, a bully's grin, cigarettes
in caretaker's cuddy, a cricket catch and rugby tally.
Kept him in that wall, and keeps him still,
but couldn't keep Pete out, and that's as present
as past as too Pete dead.
Coffin draped with football colours,
round floral tribute, kickable,
carried out as Cash sang 'Ring of Fire'.
Cremated, a rollover lottery ticket in pocket…
Typical luck!
What had that rugged kid doing scratching finger
holds in plaster cracks, after crossing half a city?
A boy's route, back of allotments, bomb site,
stagnant reservoir then wall, corridor, prep room door.
Soft knock.

Knowledge child deep drew him, and a kindly prefect
scratching at his own work, watching others,
glad of the unusual, let them speak.
Six years old, black curls, snotted, tear-stained,
knees grazed and brother hugs brother.
One teller of tales from other bed, and Pete,
tough little tacker, will not let blood be
torn from blood without this last embrace.
A father drafted and Pete for the midnight train
then flight to foreign, so must away, and he stay,
and back to prep.

Muslim Woman Floating

On an ancient sea beneath the castle tower
floats a Muslim woman clothed
from head to foot. Exotic sea borne flower,
her costume blooming and billowing
in a breeze caressing off a continent,
her burqa gently unwinding black as blood.
No idle bathe this or ritual gesture.
Hers is a deadly protest, for there's those
who'd hold her steady in a rifle sight.
Her sin? A fully clothed swim!

Nun

Nun passing, greets a woman
and her little girl, floral dressed,
blossoming hems, bucket and net.
Lays hand on head, chats, laughs.
The woman, pink and pert,
high heeled, pleated shorts,
tugs at her blouse, its elastic
bosom, nervously aware of
too much breast.
It's a day for the beach.

Fishing

I fished for shadows, reeled
in my own
like a soured, lank rag.

Drowned Fox

Fur wet, but not live wet,
greasy, steeped in sand flies,
gums white, teeth scoured,
a crusty snarl, belly bloated.
An ebbing tide tugs a frond
of seaweed flopped across gut,
almost a lover's arm but looking
like a streak of shit.

Lewis In A Tangle

Catgut tangles in its own way,
thin, tough, tightening and whitening
like cold veins into nano knot.

And there's Lewis, crew cut,
lean faced, dark earnest eyes,
picking and plucking at his lines.

Sky scudding slate grey, sun and showers,
yellow ferry bow wave bright,
and Lewis rod careful on damp gang plank.

Some secret cove, only for the tide canny,
dizzying cliff path, final sliding descent,
passed from boy to boy.
There I have him with his
catgut tangle.

Years beget years and
Lewis gone abroad, lifeguard,
beach comber, surfer, father.
Tall, still thin, found dead,
turned into his vomit,
drugs or booze or both.

The hair grows as too the nails
after death and other body
bits continue. In the modern way
they like relatives to clean and trim.

But I'll not go near,
rather walk the cliffs
where he went, think
on a boy tangle-free.

Nan

Nan, cardy shoulders hunched
against chill breeze,
stands in a scatter of toys:
yellow spade, plastic sword, deflating pool,
and other lees of a day's fun.

Dim memory moves but she frowns,
puzzled as to their use.
They smile back, late sun buoyed,
and somehow reassure.

Micro Assassin

Search no further than inwards
for the assassin:
no sure pad,
no steady glide,
nor nerveless thrust,
just a mad bastard, alias Memory.
Soon they'll upload the mind.
So what!
Invent the app can hoover up
memories that can stop you stomach kick
dead in crowded street
triggered by passing sound,
momentary glance, perfume hint;
all as real as years gone
when you pissed yourself or
betrayed her or bravado full
taunted old boy, played the troll
proud before gobby mates,
then you'll hear the applause.

The Going

We do not fear to be born,
not knowing, so fear not to die
into an adventure.
You think not?
Carve then your hand gentle
through the air, and sculpt
a cube of emptiness.
Empty? Fallacy!
A trillion atoms at a sweep,
rays, waves, gases.

Fast forward five hundred years.
What packs that cube then?
So much more and more to find.
What then do we know of
where we go when we go?

Green Grave

What territory
this dark damp forest
for canvas shrouded child,
cast in or cast out?
Curse or comfort this green giving?

Four only follow the cradled load
with heavy breath and cough,
rough funeral song to the tune of
owl's mocking hoot.

So they buried Ruba and some mason
bothered to carve a curve of pointless
steps in such daunting spot, and silly
patio, dragged a split black rock
child high for headstone.

Someone does come, across the midden,
down the badger run, through a dam of nettles
and brambles, trims leather leaves to a grave
shape, thinks to replace fungused artificial
rose, polishes the necklace of mirror bits
hanging from a board, cord inscribed
                    RUBA.
Ponders awhile, prayer or regret? Departs.

Going To The Match

On the train, leather seats,
old rolling stock,
two precise ladies
speak French.
I glean, reading my paper,
they are going to the match.
Prim, proper, older, they drink
different to the normal fan,
passing a slim silver hip flask.
Near the stadium station,
drill-like they take out
compacts and daub each cheek,
loud red, white, blue.
They look proud, more urgent –
revolutionary.

Another White Tree

They come to their tree, the cormorants,
up current tree, roots and trunk buried
in muddied water. Perch bold,
sharp yellow beaks, dog-collared,
tufted heads; spread wings to dry;
fold neat to body, torso tight,
before they squirt a shite.
Over centuries they've white shited
that tree, bole, branch – the whole lumber.

Hornpipe

On the fore deck a jaunty bugger reels,
taps hard on rise, leaps on plunge,
crazed in wild void, slab riding sea,
beneath bulbous pig's bladder of a sun –
all on auto trust.

Woodland Meeting

Strap loosened, helmet pushed back,
black, yellow stripes catching early sun,
she comes, pushing bike, muck heavy
as frost turns to mud.
Eyes bright, she smiles, they're friends,
long term, so pleasant surprise.
They talk.
She breathes rapid,
pulsing damp bosom patch
shaped firm beneath rash vest;
he sticky, over-dressed, jacket
and jumper, bobble hat pocketed.
Simple early morning walkers',
bikers' chat: shared political views,
lively love of cinema, novels, and
grey squirrels jump, a dog barks,
birds scutter, but all stills.
Fingers play on handlebars
a wisp from hers, and first
chill touch, warming gentle –
stupidity of Brexit, Coen brothers,
another McEwan or Dunm…

Brown eyes, keen lips, dimple,
icicled moustache and kiss –
long held, hidden to be hid
again for they will not
hurt with love those they love,
wait on chance or business trips.
Not dally in hard motel rooms
nor loiter in shadows of deceit.
So as they part from first, last
kiss, a decision's made, a lovers'
tryst not to love.
At barbeque or party never allow
themselves alone in kitchen or
garage. Grow wary of country walks,
chance meetings in street, shop or…
Learn you cannot live hoping the demise
of one you living love, but hope that
he, she not the first to go
might find the other.
All this tangled knowledge from
one secret woodland kiss.

Amoeba Prayer

Amoeba prayer matters
or so you've to believe
if you believe.

But if you, God, have made your universe
of Black Holes, Red Dwarves, Nuclei,
Quasars, Pulsars, Blazars, why
bother with amoeboid concerns?

So an amoeba drives off a cliff,
another goes broke,
takes a whole bunch down.
A pack of amoeba knife another,
others break up with amoeba partners –
so it goes on, amoeba moil.

Breakfast

He comes through the marble coffee tables:
white scallopy shoes, trousers to match,
peg buttoned shirt, copper medallion,
green straw hat, black band,
light grey jacket, striped red.
He's all clothes, as too
his face of patchwork,
stitched with loss and love,
faraway food and campfires.
Greets his refined friend,
red jacket, black trousers,
moccasins – neither wears socks.
In their seventies, they're still an item.

Basta!

Flint faced
long black hair
spits after him gestures
a dagger thrust pours
his coffee on the ground
gathers her bag her
broad brimmed hat
throws down coins
departs.

Casting Flowers

She braces herself,
blonde hair tumbled,
faces the sour sick sea,
and burning wind bringing
desert scorch, rapid gunfire.
Feels the suck and wet
beneath her unsuitable shoes.
Casts her flower.

Curator

Portly Arthur, slightly balding,
nods, recovers, flexes, nods again.

He curates on amongst the fisher folk
done in pink and white, dirty booted,
but clean skinned in romance style,
waiting in the well-worn way.
A fleet sailed.
A telegram pinned on the wall…
… sunk… some survivors…
… watch being kept… night
… further storms… hope…
tells all and nothing.

Arthur stirs and nods.

The women sew nets, scrub step, chide children.
A wind lifted apron helps dab eyes.

I've come to relieve you.
Ah there.
Next Saturday?
Sure thing.
Good.
I nodded off earlier, but fresher now.

Will Rising

To hell with
the sudden sprightly, on its toes
technicolored expert beyond expert
at self harm, pressing the bruising spot
as sleep becomes wake and there's
no joy cannot sorrow.
No, no, no!
Let in
the childhood cuddle,
first kiss and first goal,
the got job! Babe in arms,
sand pit play.
To hell with shit will rising.

Inflatable

A brutal bruising blast
scouring plaster, cracking brave flags,
turning bins, burning lungs and
catching breath explains the suicide,
or so it seemed.
Pale, plump apparition of ominous intent
with black slash grin, fin-backed,
bright yellow eyes,
naked, desperate to have done,
buffets pillar and balcony rail,
catches in wrought iron
flogging until flung tumbling through
palmy gardens across whipping pools,
bouncing off walls, fence, over and away –
big blob disappearing.

The Bride

At the bottom of the escalator
a gigantic bride in full flush
rushes at the commuters,
bouquet frozen in final fling,
laughing, lips pink,
teeth a dentist's delight.
So, so, so white gown bodice tight,
sleeves flounced,
skirts full and flowing,
silken slippers skipping,
in free hand a black phone palm perfect.

She's happy, free, satin sure,
bright with promise, and more.
But on her breasts in bold blue,
someone has scrawled,
"Pilgrim, I married her!"

Wound

Dagger clean and gleaming as when first done,
Memory knows no scab or bolted door
But marches steady to its own drum,
Coming on through chaos fresh and sure
As the day dear reader all changed
From love triumphant, born to thrive,
To love tamed, forced to limp, maimed.
No longer true trump, only just alive
With prison face, bruised laughter, sour sighs,
Surprise bereft, what-could-have-been eyes
But for one harsh act, never shriven,
Result of rancid revenge, passion driven,
Not forgot, when loving, lusting, afraid,
He clutched her close, thrusted and betrayed.

On The Death Of My Friend

When I think of you, old friend, pal, mate,
It's beer and trestles, pastries and pretzels,
Laughter, a jovial face and rolling gait.
We were well met, knew to let the world go fret,
Tell a tale, break a jest, eat full, drink late.

So take your rest, your well-earned ease,
Me? I'll cast a flower upon the seas,
Think on two old boys, a pint, a bench
Where we'd have sat. In the bag. Cracked it!
No more clocks, ticking boxes, hacked it!

But now strange space, untimely wrench.
Me? Forget it. I'll be just fine.
Bite the olive, sip the wine.
Think how we were blessed,
Until we meet again… I'll do my best.

Spy

It took a certain sort of spy, Berlin 1960s,
and Michaels two weeks in wasn't
certain he was it. Knew his craft,
done the training, but now descending
the gouged damp steps beneath a
weary metro sign – he'd changed his
route, no lapsing into routine –
felt like descending into a sewer,
seeping brickwork, cold handrail,
dark arches and the platform,
Geisterbahn if ever.
Scared? Just a bristle, not
the sudden reflux, or churning
urge to shit but…
A woman headscarfed, heavy overcoated,
slowly stamped;
a man, lank long rain coat, wide brimmed hat,
studied a torn advert.
He did some thinking in Russian for practise,
shuffled his feet, punched gloved hands together,
forgot the word for –
"*Haben Sie Feur bitte?*"
Hell, did he come from?
"*Ja.*"
Teeth removing glove, fumbling,
spilled a match, flare.
Cheap rolled, spit ruined cigarette,

leaning in, eyes half closed, unshaven,
whiff of sour stew, clasps wrist, cold, strong.
Black nailed thumb on finger douses flame,
"*Willkommen in Berlin Herr Michaels.*"
Gone!

On The Tube

Turquoise trainers, rainbow socks,
black tights, quilted jacket,
straight black hair either side of her round
Asiatic bespectacled face, black frames.
Gently, balletically,
she exercises holding
the yellow bar in the middle of the carriage rattling us under
London.

One-Man Universe

He sleeps in the back of a van,
washes in streams, fries in a can,
has a body all motley,
a tattooed scene
of every creature he's been –
all poise precise and true
awaiting their cue –
for with a churn of his elbows
and knock of his knees
it's hustle and bustle
at command of his muscle,
a circus at work,
a menagerie gone beserk.

Old

An old man
in the corner
speaks to a cactus.
The one leathery, fibrous, thorny,
the other just a plant.

Squashed At The Station

Huddled over her Kindle,
rucksack, plastic bag, suede boots,
she's cold, hands deep in purple jacket,
thighs clenched, scrunched forward,
nodding prayer-like. At intervals
a furtive hand touches the screen.
Beside her an elderly gent
awkwardly folds his Telegraph,
stands, long scarf and rich coat,
steps away, a passport falls.
Excuse me. Mr! Sir!
Oh thank you. I'm so grateful.
A woman squeezes
through, on phone, picking
past bags and cases,
that is nuts, absolute nuts,
husky voice and gone.

A Promise

The house we built is full of mocks tonight,
a ghost's chilled derision of all we did
and as I lie in the hearse of your midnight absence
made worse by the lees of your perfume
then I could go, were it not for
a promise made.

Information Desk

One glossy morning,
a blue brochured sky
as crisp as fresh plastic,
short-staffed,
no point Eric idling
his beat of litter done,
heavy mug in hand.
Put him on the info stand.

Alone in main concourse,
it took his curdled brain,
product of a biker's skid,
a while to get the hang
but after staring blandly
at jolly pamphlets,
tight timetables
through yellow crusted eyes,
fingering the draining tube
around his ear,
with broad grin, missing tooth,
he began.

Delighted in rhythm and rush
of crowd and crush,
dispatched throngs to platforms
and destinations not planned.
Who knows what near
misses met, what ships
didn't pass that night?

And still now and then
mopping a cubicle,
he cocks an ear, hopes for station master's call,
Eric take the info stall.

Late Infidelity

So what if she slept years ago
with a colleague? So what!
Me no innocent. So why
in this eighties time when living
is by the day, care?
Because life and love's a fucker!
Liar! It's pride.
The wasting pride of a flaccid penis
and waning libido.
Give over. No one is property.
So why should my feelings,
lurching towards crematorium,
matter?

Doves

We need the magic man, the one
who on a smooth pass can fill
commuter carriage with doves
white, grey, pink,
jewel-eyed, dignified.

Doves on floor, doves on seats,
doves on racks, fitted and packed
in gentle shifting bustle, cooing choir,
mournful and haunting, bringing
the guard, scornful and daunting.

The magic man claps and
he, the guard, is a flourish of feathers,
shoulders plumed and preened
mouth beaked, coat tail peaked.

Tickets please, more a squawk
or sudden squeak,
as a hundred migrate specials
with a sleight of hand appear in a fan.

Old Love

Given the state of play,
I'd say
Your man's a lemon.
The only state can explain
Why with more years than most
He'd embark on love.
Aren't slime covered stepping stones
Enough?

Boat

The boat is blind
but brisk, energetic,
knowing nothing of shoal,
overfall, rocky outcrop or
instruments down, vis dropping.

A shining bow wave,
all jewel and sparkle,
dolphin-backed, lit within,
curving iridescent
in smooth seeping dark
speaks a jaunty insouciance.
But
boats only seem alive
with a good cracking wind,
canvas proud, shrouds straining.
They would not hesitate
to self destruct.

And
on a night like this,
the wanted flashing light
not where it should be
they are treacherous.
The promise of we'll make it
whispering away in every
roll and plunge is false.
For
it's all down to you.

Glass Of Water

Fingertip moist, cold,
standing on sun mottled
table top – the glass.
Sudden, silent, soft
on surface – the leaf.
Sip by sip it sinks
and moulds on to
glossy chunk of ice.

Last Thought

Well tumoured, buggered and battered,
watching a drip feed's silky flow.
So it's come to this.
Death's breath is not chill,
but clammy and antiseptic.
Where now the rapier thrust,
the whoop and slick escape,
the last words?
Lost in the starchy comfort of a
nodding nurse's neon light… Come give me the drink.

The Senderos

Theirs the incident, theirs the muse:
peak encrusted sky, hawk caught cry,
troubador song, goat moan, hearth crackle,
surf rip, picnic litter, nervous neigh,
inn rustic, cave home, ruined wall,
hiker's sticks, oily rag, plastic bottle:

all made for mind's wander as
solitary flower becomes buttonhole,
bridesmaid's delight, proud suitor's
nervous gesture, and then –

a wilting flower by patient's side
lonely witness to one just died –

arrived! To part again,
other moods, new voices:
a pilgrim proud? A cigar butt?
Those dregs upon a bar,

her face over coffee and cake, serene.
How triggered by a corpse crow clean?

So the constant surprise of
the teasing sun beaten,
storm sodden senderos.

What's that?
Cuckoo call, cunning trickster?
No,
it's the never ending poetic whisper.

Thanks

To Philip Sealey for his friendship, advice, support and praise, Alan Sanigar for artistic advice, Marlie Strike for help with cover design, and finally Dominic, Kate and family for coming into my life.

Matador

For exclusive discounts on Matador titles,
sign up to our occasional newsletter at
troubador.co.uk/bookshop